HOW TO DRAW
Ballet Pictures

Barbara Soloff Levy

Dover Publications, Inc.
Mineola, New York

Note

A ballerina spins across the stage. Her partner leaps into the air—higher than it seems possible. These dancers are part of the great tradition of classical ballet, the subject of this delightful book. Using thirty step-by-step instruction pages, you will learn to draw ballet dancers, as well as a variety of dance steps (such as the five basic positions of the feet and arms), outfits, scenes from famous ballets, and many other aspects of this exciting dance form. You will learn how to say some French ballet terms, too.

Each instruction page has three or four steps. First, draw the basic shapes in step one. For the remaining steps, you will add details to your picture. The last step shows you the finished drawing. It's a good idea to trace the steps first, just to get a feel for drawing. There's also a Practice Page with plenty of space opposite each picture. Use a pencil with an eraser in case you want to make any changes along the way. You will see dotted lines in some of the pictures—you can erase these lines as a final step. When you are pleased with your drawing, you may wish to go over the lines with a felt-tip pen or colored pencil. Finally, feel free to color your drawings any way you wish.

After you have finished the drawings in this book, why not use your imagination to create new pictures of your very own? Let's begin!

Bibliographical Note

How to Draw Ballet Pictures is a new work, first published by Dover Publications, Inc., in 2009.

International Standard Book Number

ISBN-13: 978-0-486-47055-9
ISBN-10: 0-486-47055-5

Manufactured in the United States of America
Dover Publications, Inc., 31 East 2nd Street, Mineola, N.Y. 11501

HOW TO DRAW
Ballet Pictures

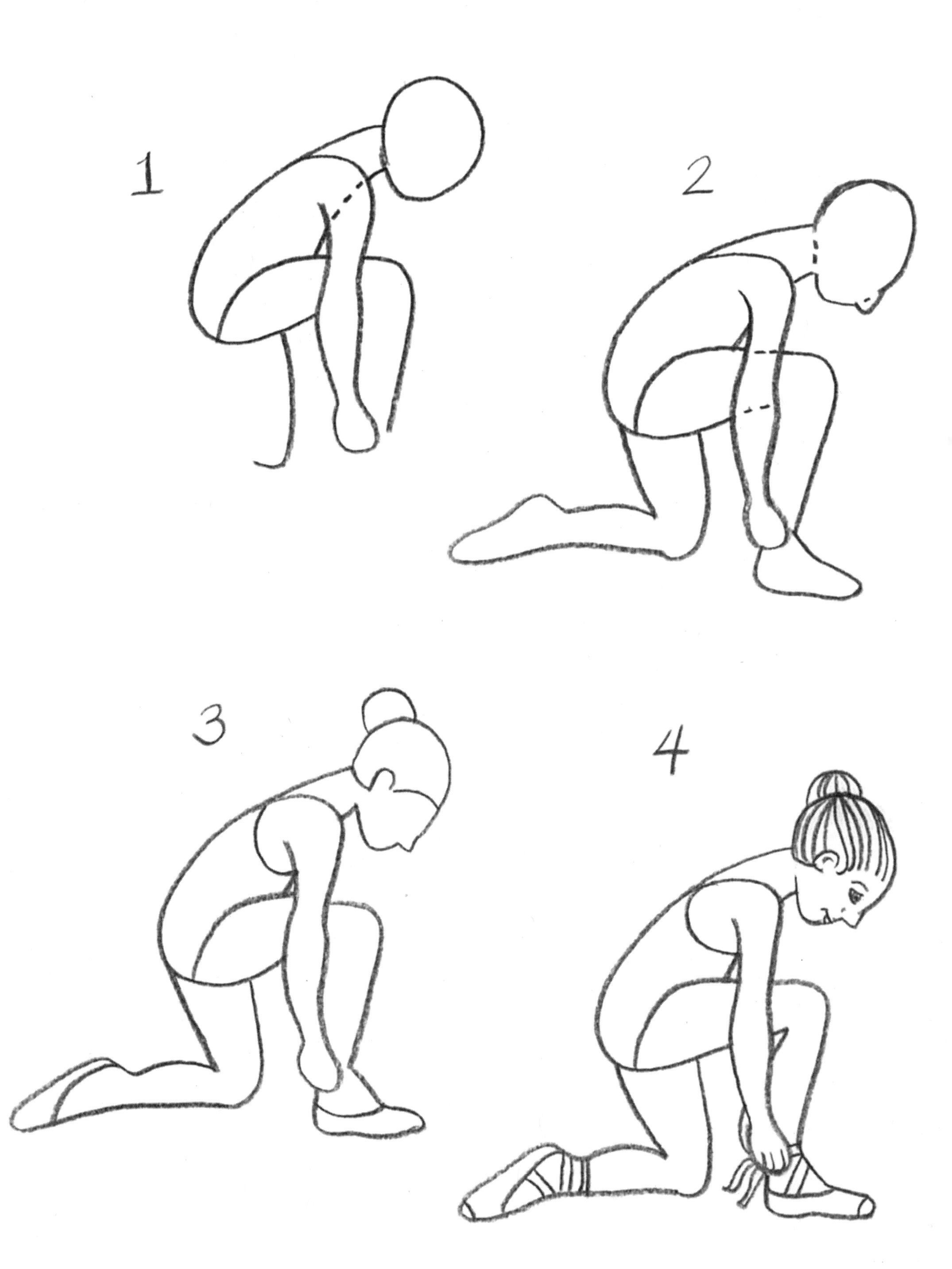
1
2
3
4

Practice Page

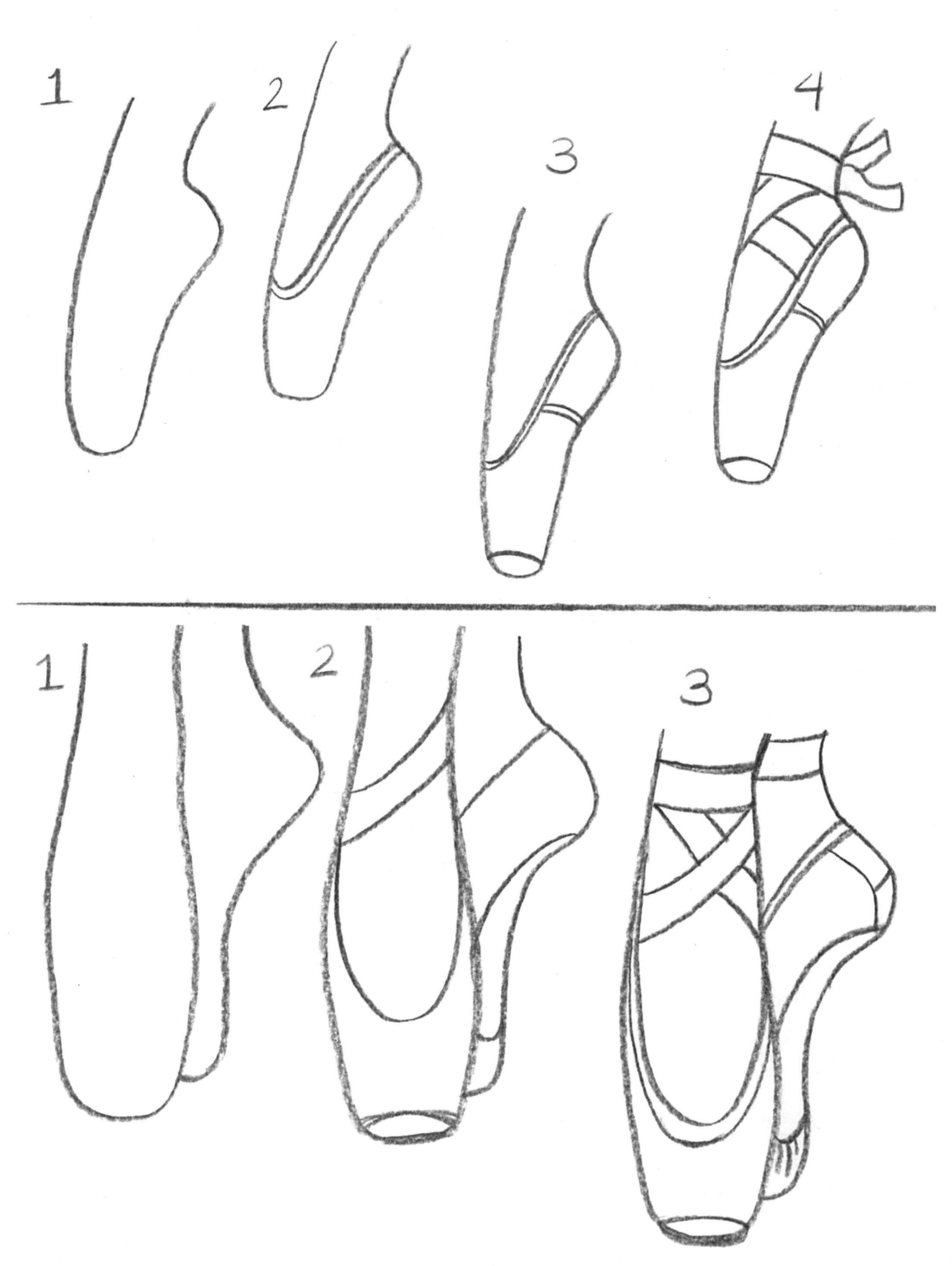
1
2
3
4
1
2
3

Practice Page

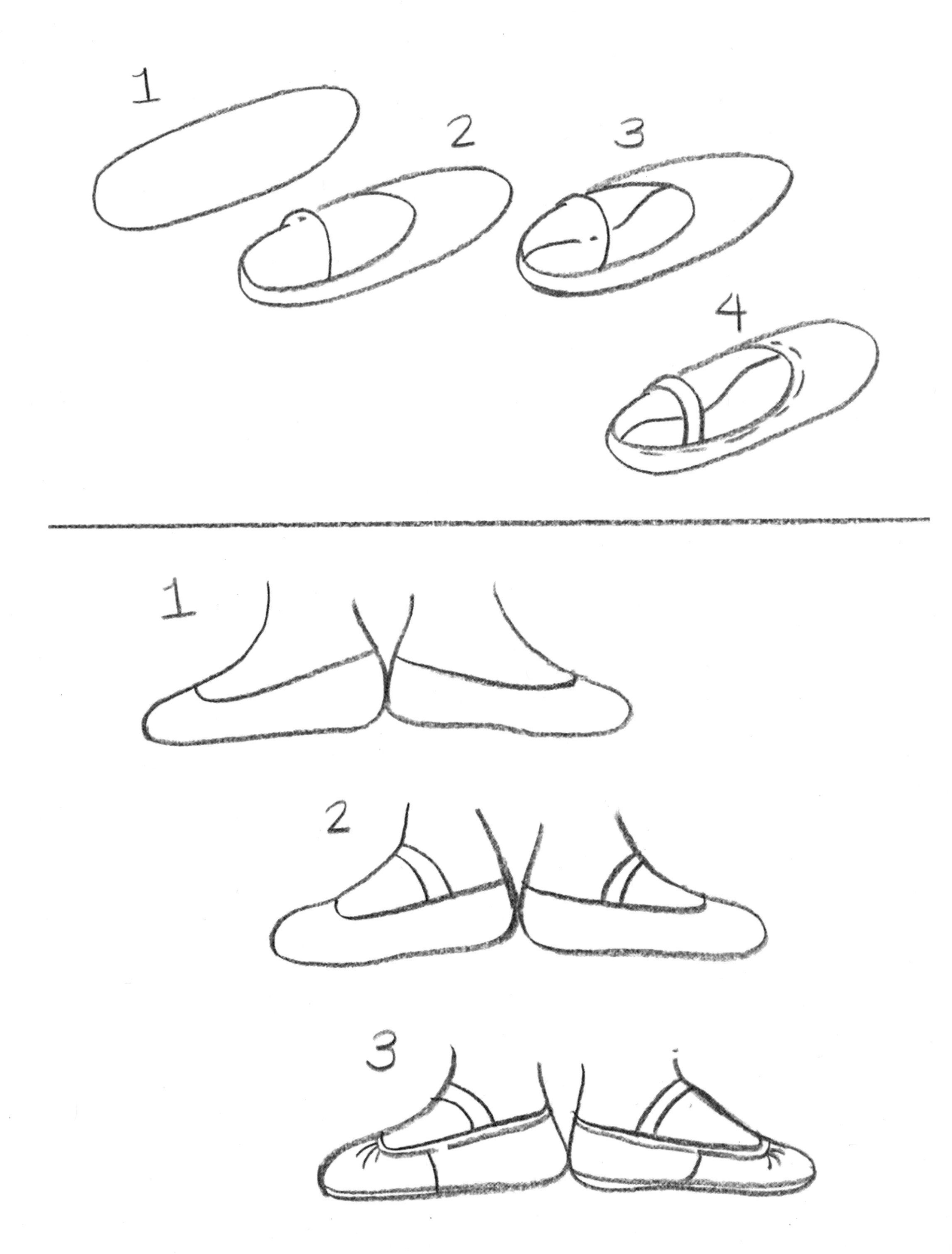
1
2
3
4
1
2
3

Practice Page

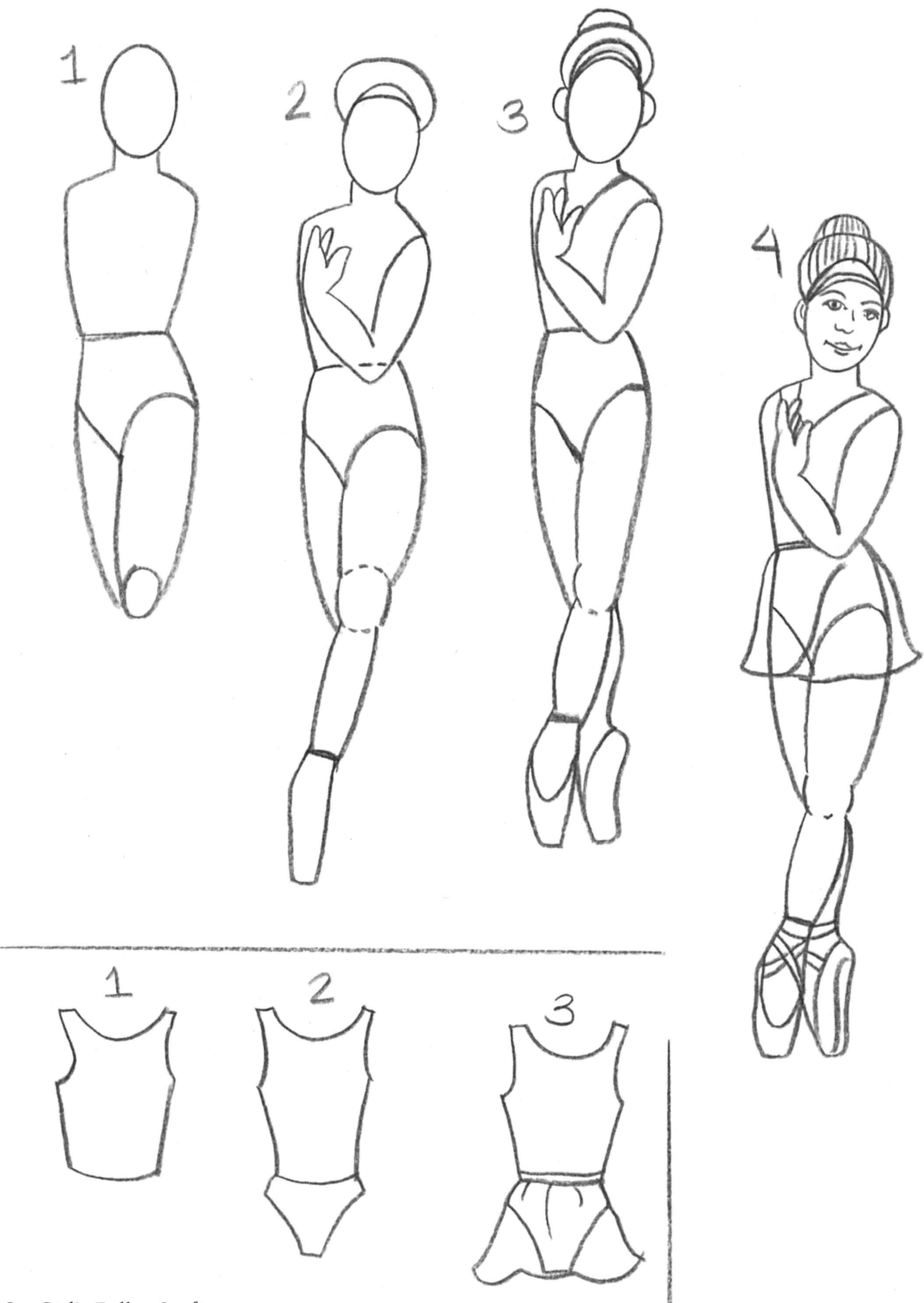
1
2
3
4
1
2
3

Practice Page

1
2
3
1
2
3
1
2
3

Practice Page

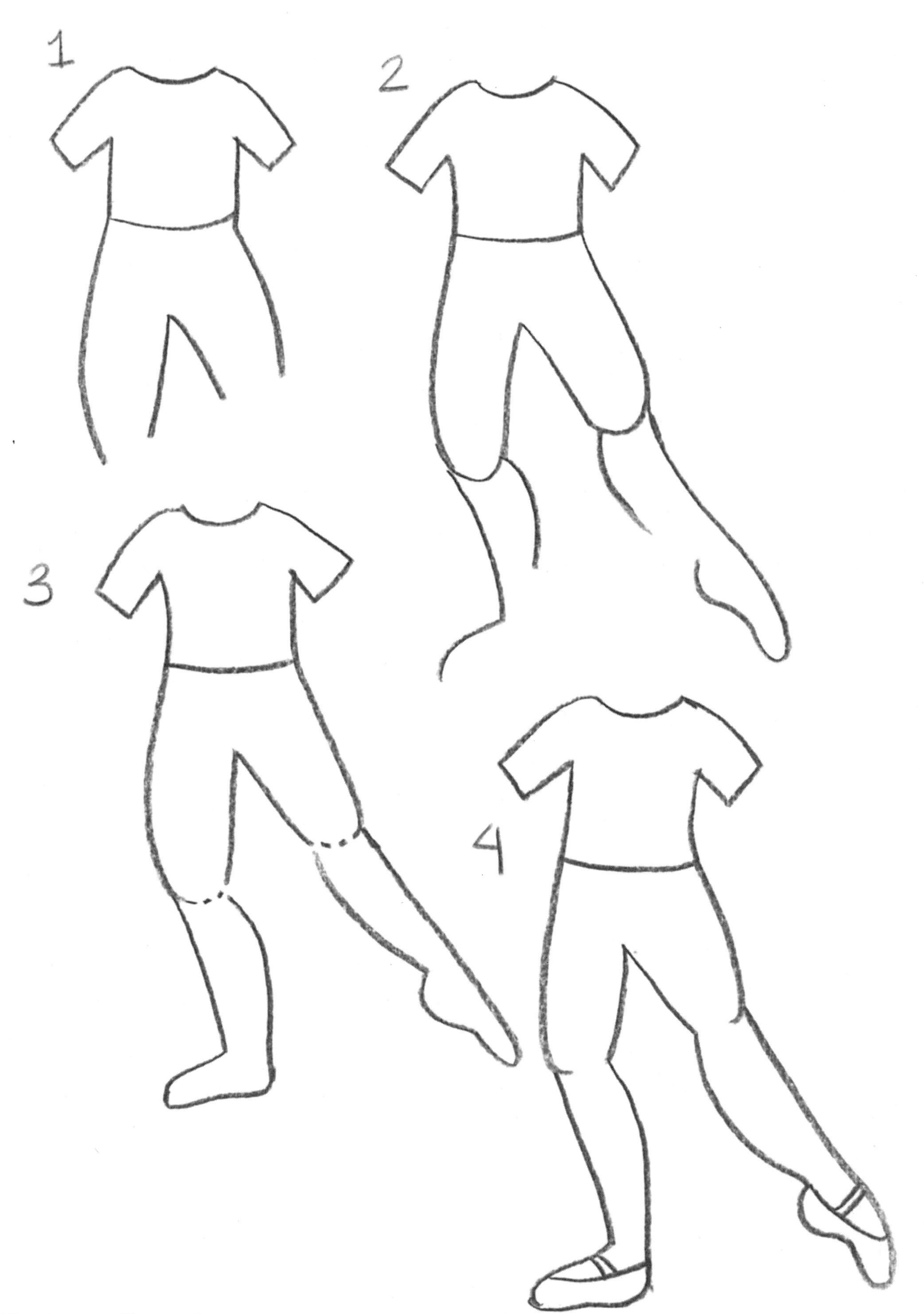
1
2
3
4

Practice Page

1
2

3
4

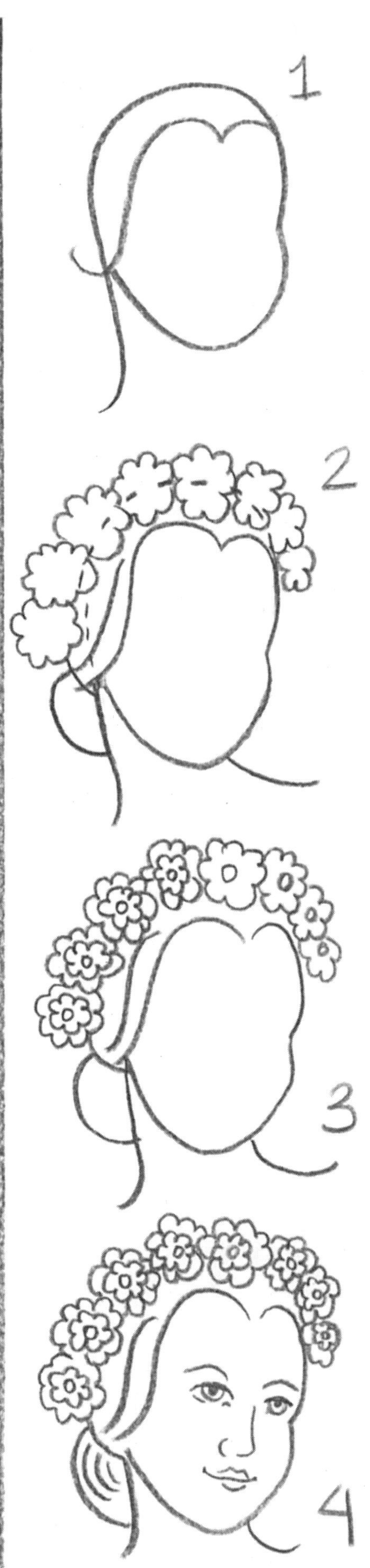
1
2
3
4

Practice Page

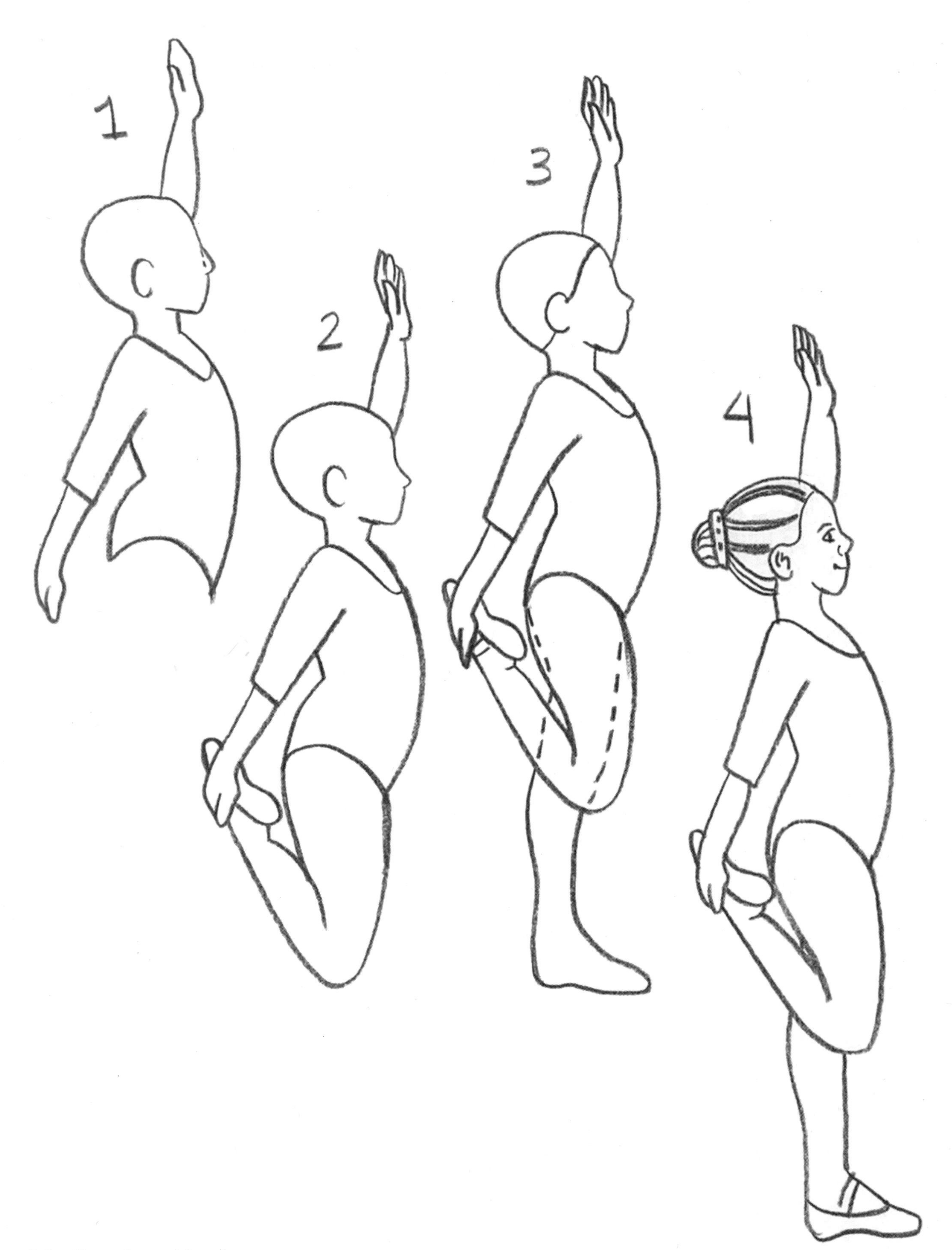
1
2
3
4

Practice Page

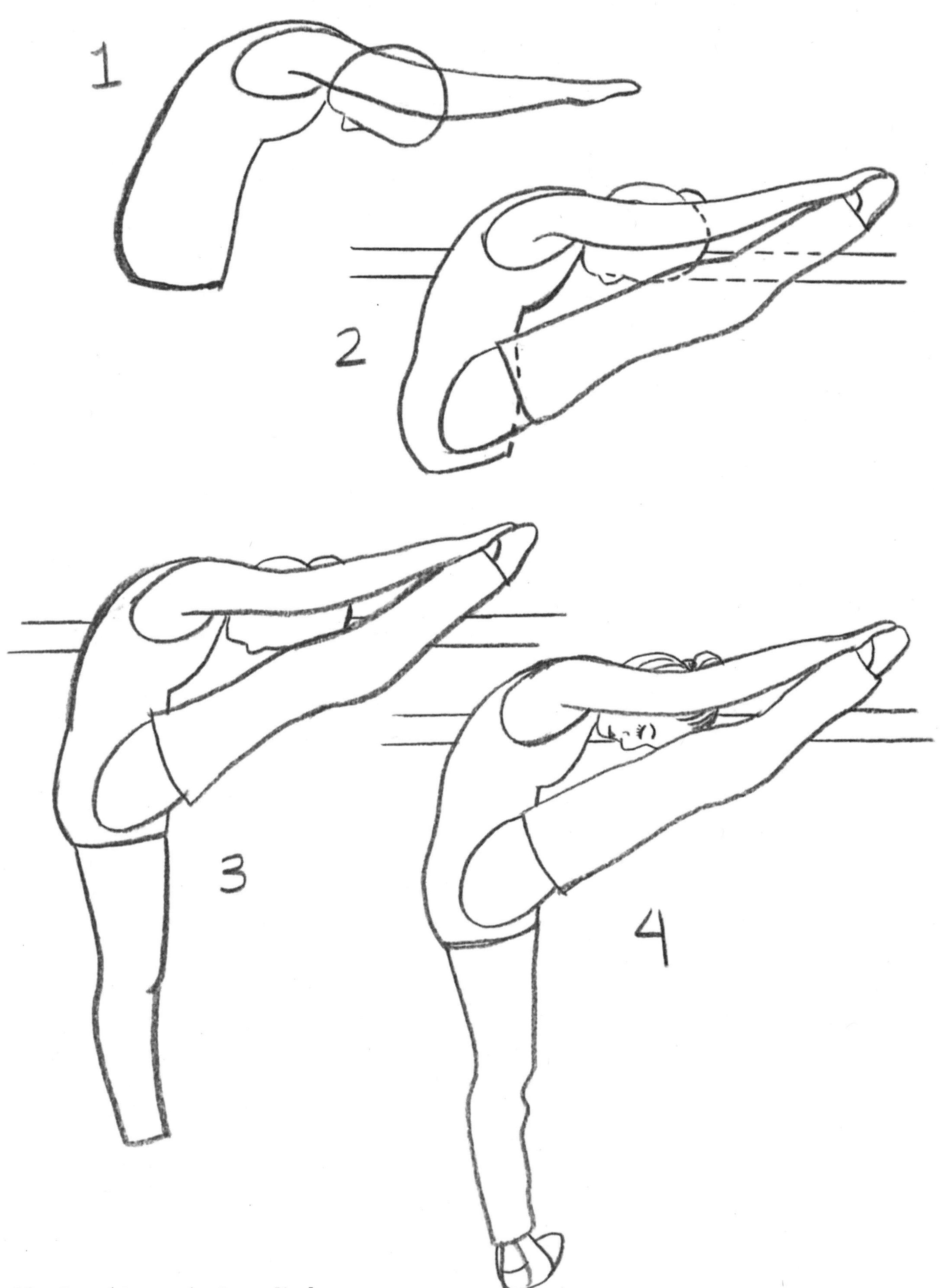
1
2
3
4

Practice Page

1
2
3
4

Practice Page

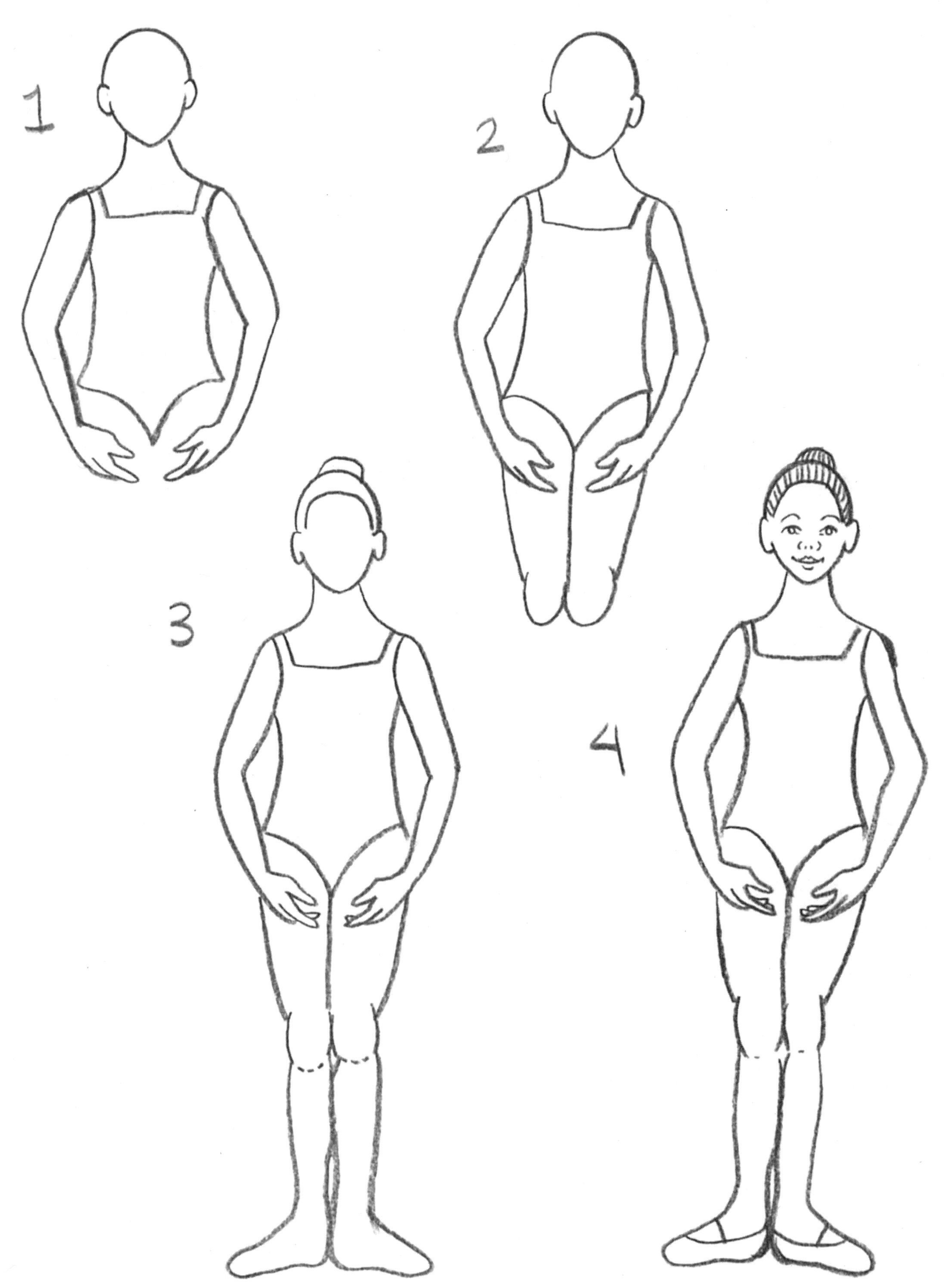
1
2
3
4

Practice Page

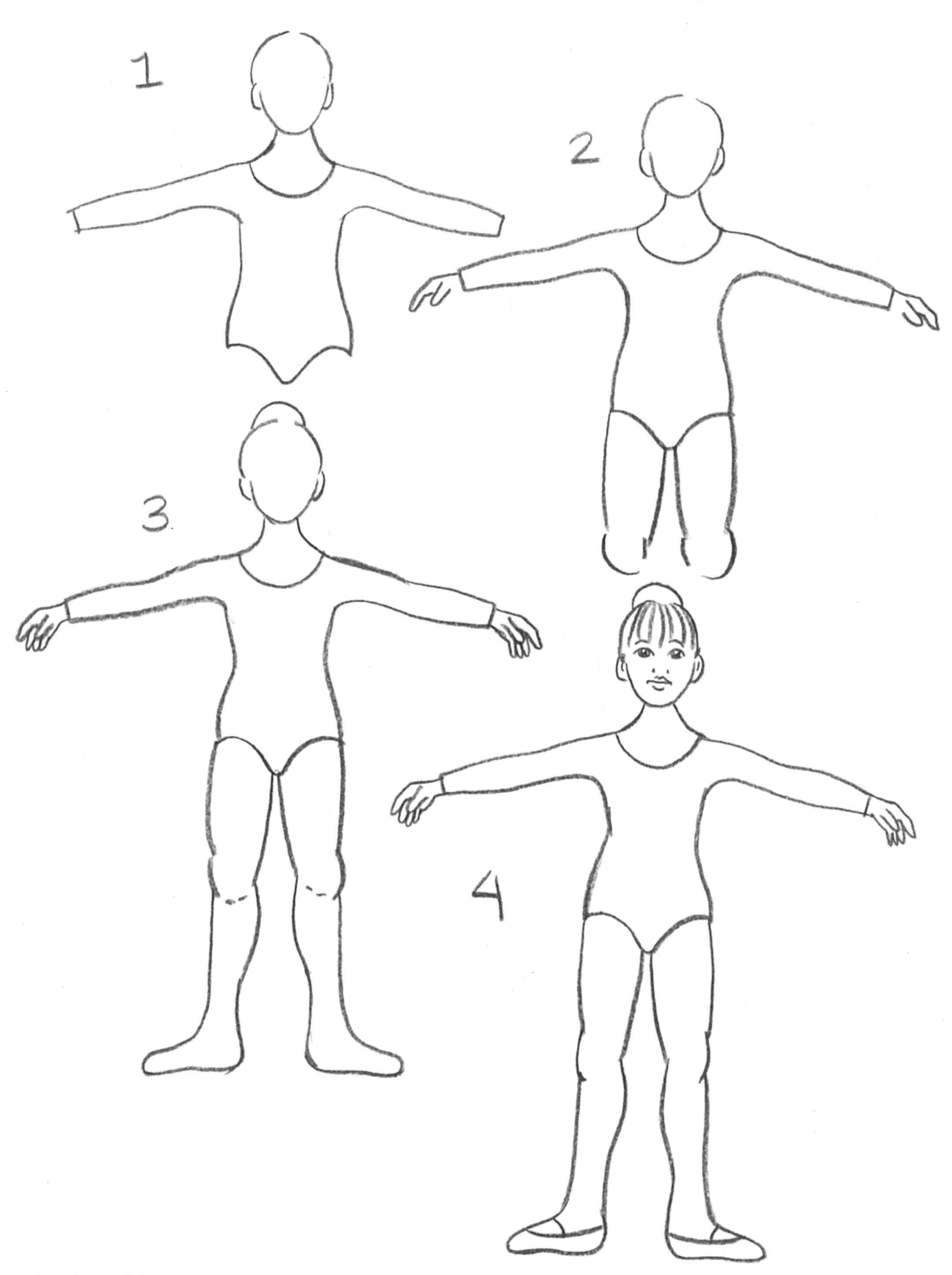
1
2
3
4

Practice Page

1
2
3
4

Practice Page

1
2
3
4

Practice Page

1
2
3
4

Practice Page

 Pas de Bourrée [***pah*** *duh bore-**ay***]

Practice Page

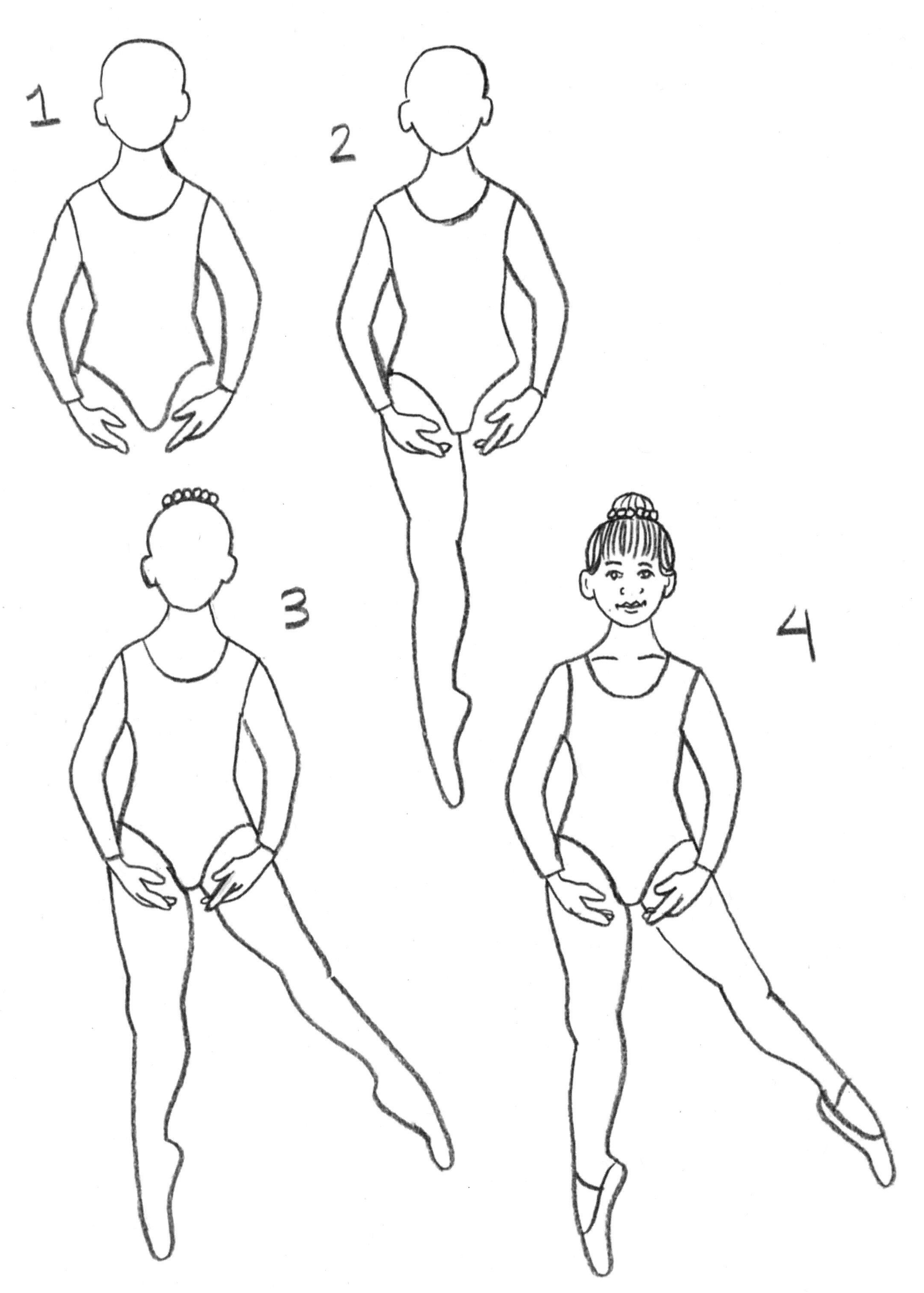
1
2
3
4

Practice Page

1
2
3
4

Practice Page

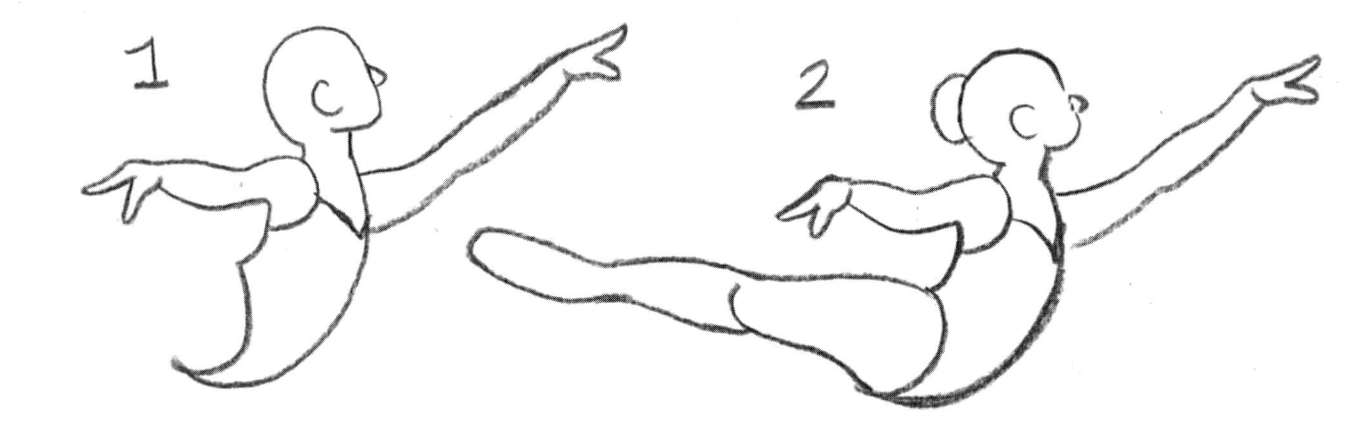
1
2

3
4

Practice Page

1

2

3

4

Practice Page

1
2
3
4

Practice Page

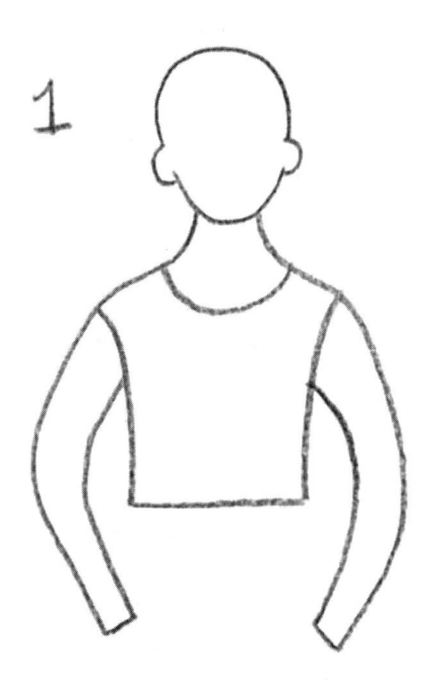
1

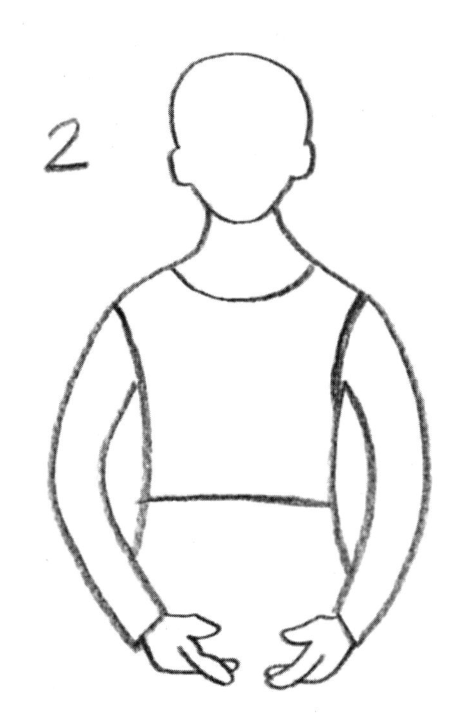
2

3

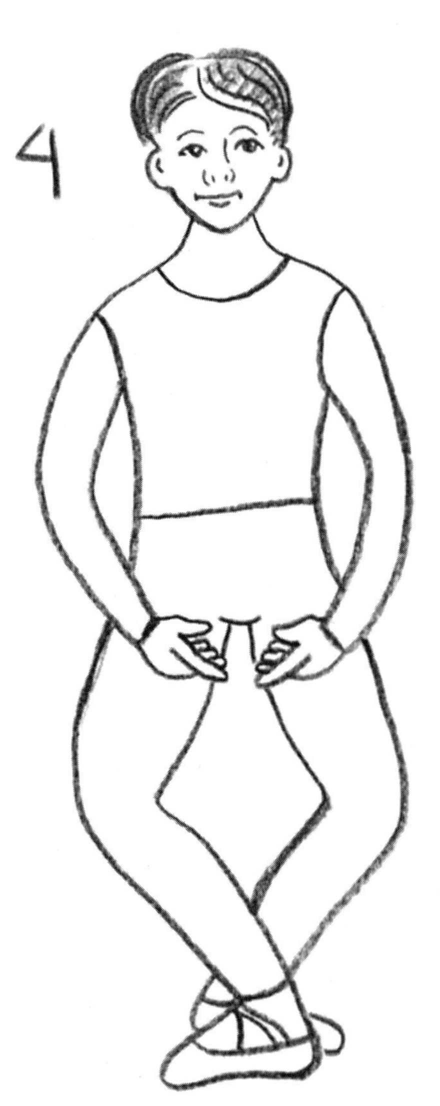
4

Practice Page

1
2
3
4

Practice Page

1

2

3

4

Practice Page

1
2
3
4

Practice Page

1
2
3
4

Practice Page

1
2
3
4

Practice Page

1
2
3
4

Practice Page

1
2
3
4

Practice Page

1
2
3
4

Practice Page